Best wishes for good health
to

_____

from

_____

date

_____

# The Get-Well BOOK

*Compiled by Anna Trimiew*

Harold Shaw Publishers
Wheaton, Illinois

Copyright © 1996 by Harold Shaw Publishers

Cover design by David LaPlaca
Compiled by Anna Trimiew

ISBN 0-87788-243-6

**Library of Congress Cataloging-in-Publication Data**

The get-well book for people on the mend / compiled by Anna Trimiew.
     p.    cm.
  ISBN 0-87788-243-6
  1. Sick—Prayer-books and devotions—English.  2. Consolation—Quotations, maxims, etc.
  3. Consolation—Biblical teaching.  4. Bible—Quotations.   I. Trimiew, Anna, 1948-
BV4905.2.G48  1996
242'.4—dc20                                          96-26386
                                                        CIP

05  04  03  02  01  00  99  98  97  96

10  9  8  7  6  5  4  3  2  1

# CONTENTS

## Songs and Sunshine for the Soul

## Something to Live By

# Acknowledgments

We have sought to secure permissions for all copyrighted material in this book. Where copyright holders could not be located or acknowledgment was inadvertently omitted, the publisher expresses its regret.

The following lyrics by James Ward are used by permission:

"Faith Is What You Hope For," copyright 1980 Music Anno Domini (A.D.). All rights reserved.
"Buckled Over," copyright 1974 Music Anno Domini (A.D.). All rights reserved.
"No Bad News," copyright 1980 Music Anno Domini (A.D.). All rights reserved.
"Keep Looking Up," copyright 1981 Music Anno Domini (A.D.). All rights reserved.

All Scripture quotations, unless otherwise indicated, are taken from the *Holy Bible, New International Version.* Copyright © 1973, 1978, 1984 by International Bible Society. Used by permission of Zondervan Publishing House. All rights reserved. The "NIV" and "New International Version" trademarks are registered in the United States Patent and Trademark Office by International Bible Society. Use of either trademark requires permission of International Bible Society.

Scripture quotations marked KJV are from the *King James Version* of the Bible.

Scripture quotations marked TLB are from *The Living Bible,* copyright © 1971. Used by permission of Tyndale House Publishers, Inc., Wheaton, IL 60189. All rights reserved.

Scripture quotations marked NKJV are from *The New King James Version.* Copyright © 1979, 1980, 1982 Thomas Nelson Inc., Publishers.

Scripture quotations marked NRSV are from the *New Revised Standard Version* of the Bible, copyrighted 1989 by the Division of Christian Education of the National Council of the Churches of Christ in the United States of America, and are used by permission. All rights reserved.

Scripture quotations marked RSV are from the *Revised Standard Version* of the Bible, copyright 1946, 1952, 1971 by the Division of Christian Education of the National Council of the Churches of Christ in the U.S.A., and used by permission. All rights reserved.

# HOPE FOR RECOVERY

# Faith That Makes a Difference

A person's view of what can be done with life may be measured by a person's faith.

*Edgar N. Jackson,* Conquering Disability

But they that wait upon the LORD shall renew their strength; they shall mount up with wings as eagles; they shall run, and not be weary; and they shall walk, and not faint.

*Isaiah 40:31, KJV*

My faith in God and myself became most important to me. I knew I didn't want or need to be sick—I just was. And I started dealing with it one day at a time. I found a place of peace and comfort in the midst of my uncertainty.

*Linda Hanner, John J. Witek, M.D., with Robert B. Clift, Ph.D.,*
When You're Sick and Don't Know Why

Faith gives us the courage to face the present with confidence, and the future with expectancy.

*Anonymous*

Because God is who he is and has such an impeccable character, we may be utterly sure our confidence in him, our faith in him, will never be betrayed. What a tonic for tension!

*W. Phillip Keller,* Taming Tension

Is anyone among you suffering? He should keep on praying about it. . . . Is anyone sick? He should call for the elders of the church and they should pray over him and pour a little oil upon him, calling on the Lord to heal him. And their prayer, if offered in faith, will heal him, for the Lord will make him well; and if his sickness was caused by some sin, the Lord will forgive him.

*James 5:13-15,* TLB

Faith is the daring of the soul to go farther than it can see.

*Anonymous*

I've read the last page of the Bible. It's all going to turn out all right.

*Billy Graham*

She [Lady Victoria Buxton] was struck down suddenly, a lovely young wife and mother, in February 1869, and held fast by "searching and exhausting" pain till July 1916. Forty-seven years of pain. And yet her life was one of valorous patience, forgetfulness of self, service to others; and such a sense of light was about her.

*Amy Carmichael*, Rose from Brier

Waiting patiently in expectation is the foundation of the spiritual life.

*Simone Weil*, First and Last Notebooks

Sometimes God, in a mercy which we cannot comprehend, has to deliberately compel us to take an enforced rest for a season. Illness, sudden reverses, or chilling circumstances come like the dark, cold grip of winter upon a Christian, compelling him to cease from his busyness.

*W. Phillip Keller*, As a Tree Grows

Phyllis thought it a very bad sign that Americans were so afraid of pain that they thought the worst thing in the world was to suffer. She felt suffering had brought her back to God, back to a real understanding of what was important in the world.

Phyllis claimed that the Spirit of God came to her in the night and comforted her. She said it was like a warm light and that it gave her an overwhelming feeling that all shall be well, and all manner of things shall be well.

*Daniel Taylor,* Letters to My Children

Growing in faith is not so much like going through stages as it is like exploring a new country. . . . There is always more to be seen and understood and taken in.

*Craig R. Dykstra*

It is not always easy to simply step aside into solitude and rest and quietness. But unless I learn how, my entire growth in God will be endangered.

*Keller,* As a Tree Grows

Prayer gives strength to the weak, faith to the fainthearted, and courage to the fearful.

*Anonymous*

My first steps were fun, but it still seemed very hard. I'd say it was about eight or nine months from the amputations to when I first started to walk. Then it was another two weeks before I could walk up and down stairs, then it was about a year before I learned to run. Now I don't even have to think about it. Now I jump, I leap, I gallop.

*Adam Jed, quoted in* I Will Sing Life: Voices from the Hole in the Wall Gang Camp
*by Larry Berger, Dahlia Lithwick, and Seven Campers*

I once called life a "beautiful burden," and someone got mad at me for calling it a burden. But I think it is like an enormous gift that is handed to you that may be hard to carry, and you may need some help carrying it.

*Bernie S. Siegel, M.D.,* How to Live between Office Visits

Come to me, all you who are weary and burdened, and I will give you rest. Take my yoke upon you and learn from me, for I am gentle and humble in heart, and you will find rest for your souls. For my yoke is easy and my burden is light.

*Matthew 11:28-30*

God is stronger than fire and destruction, and even in the valleys of deepest darkness, rod and staff are put into our hands and bridges are thrown across the abyss.

*Helmut Thielicke*

Hope is putting faith to work when doubting would be easier.

*Anonymous*

Spirituality is a healing force.

*Siegel,* How to Live between Office Visits

He is Jesus, the Christ . . . the suffering Savior who was a man of sorrows and acquainted with grief—our sort of grief. He did not come to condemn the world but to redeem it; He did not come to judge us but to lift us up. His main mission was to bind up the brokenhearted, to set free captives, to comfort all that mourn, to give beauty in place of ashes and the oil of joy and garment of praise in place of heavy spirits.

*Keller,* Taming Tension

# The Path of Healing

I hope when I get well it will be better, I'll be able to go back to feeling like I can just be myself. But once you've lived through something that is life or death like this, some things are going to seem trivial. And you never lose that.

*Tina Kenney, quoted in* I Will Sing Life

Despise no new accident in your body, but ask opinion of it.

*Francis Bacon*

Develop a sense of humor. This can be a most valuable asset. Have a good laugh every day, even if the situation is ridiculous.

*Anthony B. Montapert*

For the doctor, illness and trauma are a challenge to practice the healing skills. For the chaplain, they represent opportunities to make real the presence of God as a God who loves all of His creatures, not a God of judgment or detachment.

*Kushner,* Who Needs God

We'd all like to feel self-reliant and capable of coping with whatever adversity comes our way, but that's not how most human beings are made. It's my belief that the capacity to accept help is inseparable from the capacity to give help when our turn comes to be strong.

*Fred Rogers*, You Are Special

For I will restore health to you, and your wounds I will heal, says the Lord.

*Jeremiah 30:17, NRSV*

The best cure for the body is a quiet mind.

*Napoleon Bonaparte*

For on a certain evening there was special prayer for the healing touch, and that night the pain was lulled and natural sleep was given. The blissfulness of the awakening next morning is still vivid and shining. I lay for a few minutes almost wondering if I were still on earth.

*Carmichael*, Rose from Brier

Some of my richest experiences have come out of the most painful times . . . those that were the hardest to believe would ever turn into anything positive.

*Rogers*, You Are Special

You can groan and suffer in this fallen world, yet you can learn to rejoice. You can learn to triumph in your hope, in your tribulations and the good things they produce in your life—and above all, in God Himself.

*Myers,* 31 Days of Praise

When I was at the worst point of my illness and in the midst of a suicidal depression, if anyone had told me that life would someday be good again, I could not have believed it. But they would have been right.

*Hanner et al.,* When You're Sick and Don't Know Why

The physician is not solving a crossword: he is performing a delicate, adventurous, and experimental creative act, of which the patient's body is the material, and to which the creative co-operation of the patient's will is necessary. He is not rediscovering a state of health, temporarily obscured; he is remaking it, or rather, helping it to remake itself.

*Dorothy L. Sayers,* The Mind of the Maker

Always fall in with what you're asked to accept. Take what is given, and make it over your way. My aim in life has always been to hold my own with whatever's going. Not against: with.

*Robert Frost, quoted in* Good Advice, *by Leonard Safir and William Safire*

The patient's best way to health and peace of mind is to enter with understanding into the nature of the physician's task. If he does so, he will not only be better placed to cooperate creatively with him, but he will be relieved from the mental misery of impatience and frustration.

*Sayers,* Mind of the Maker

The art of living is more like that of wrestling than of dancing; the main thing is to stand firm and be ready for an unforeseen attack.

*Marcus Aurelius*

If thy strength will serve, go forward in the ranks; if not, stand still.

*Confucian proverb*

Dwell not upon thy weariness; thy strength shall be according to the measure of thy desire.

*Arab proverb*

Drag your thoughts away from your troubles—by the ears, by the heels, or any other way, so you manage it; it's the healthiest thing a body can do.

*Mark Twain*

One of the most sublime experiences we can ever have is to wake up feeling healthy after we have been sick. Even if it is only relief from a headache or toothache, the health we take for granted most of the time is suddenly seen to be an incredible blessing. If we credit this return to health to our own recuperative powers or to the wonders of modern medicine, it will be just another encounter with technology in our lives, one more instance of idol-worship. But if we see the return to health as an encounter with God . . . then we make room in our lives for reverence.

*Kushner,* Who Needs God

Take care of your health. If you have it, thank God, and value it next to a sound mind.

*Anonymous*

Consider well what your strength is equal to, and what exceeds your ability.

*Horace*

He who has health is rich and does not know it.

*Italian proverb*

# Treasures from Within

Patience is the best remedy for every trouble.

*Plautus*

This is my comfort in my affliction, for your word has given me life.

*Psalm 119:50, NKJV*

On the way back from dinner one night, Pia suggested to a group of campers and counselors, "Let's all start laughing for no reason at all, until we realize how silly we're being, and that makes us start really laughing." It worked, and Pia laughed the longest and hardest. She has become an expert at producing joy out of nowhere. For seventeen years, she has lived with a severe case of sickle cell anemia and with poverty, and yet she is most famous at camp for her stories that make people laugh.

*Larry Berger et al., I Will Sing Life*

To miss the joy is to miss all.

*Robert Louis Stevenson*

Weeping may remain for a night, but rejoicing comes in the morning.

*Psalm 30:5*

Hope is what keeps us going in any adverse situation.

*Hanner et al.,* When You're Sick and Don't Know Why

Take away the many fears, suspicions, and doubts by which I prevent you from being my Lord, and give me the courage and freedom to appear naked and vulnerable in the light of your presence, confident in your unfathomable mercy.

*Henri Nouwen,* A Cry for Mercy

I am astonished at her, the good mother. She has called me to her sickbed, not so much to help her as to help me. I, in childhood, was never hungry, never homeless, never seriously ill; and was never exposed to the sight of physical suffering. My parents had made sure of all that. But an easy ride of a life is only a half-truth. Now Mama's gift is to let me know her pain.

*Lois F. Lyles, "Waiting on the Sick," in* Double Stitch, *edited by Patricia Bell-Scott and others*

The winterfallowed heart readies itself for gifts whenever they come.

*Martin E. Marty,* A Cry of Absence

Even in troubled circumstances, or when God does not choose to work in spectacular ways, praise can help us view our situation through different lenses. It can help produce within us a restful, invigorating inner climate.

*Myers,* 31 Days of Praise

Do not pray for ease. Pray for strength to bear the burden.

*Anonymous*

Never apologize for showing feeling. When you do so, you apologize for truth.

*Benjamin Disraeli*

Facing life's realities, its downs as well as its ups, is one kind of daily courage we all must learn.

*William J. Bennett,* The Book of Virtues

Do not measure your loss by itself; if you do, it will seem intolerable; but if you take all human affairs into account you will find that some comfort is to be derived from them.

*Saint Basil*

Never think that God's delays are God's denials. Hold on; hold fast; hold out. Patience is genius.

*Comte de Buffon*


You are my hiding place; you will protect me from trouble and surround me with songs of deliverance.

*Psalm 32:7*


Life's field will yield as we make it
A harvest of thorns or of flowers.

*Johann Wolfgang von Goethe, "Perseverance," quoted in* The Book of Virtues


The imagination is even more powerful than a tumor. A tumor can only grow certain ways. It depends on the cancer and what stage you're in. But the imagination grows wonders. I don't know the limit of mine and I probably never will—it can't be limited. Imagination can go everywhere, it's a way of life and life can't end because there's something after life. But a tumor has limits—if it grows too big, it won't have nothing to grow on. If you look at the imagination and the tumor—one soars and the other gets stuck in the body.

*Corey Svien, in* I Will Sing Life

O Lord Jesus Christ, you who forgave the sins of the paralytic before you let him walk again . . . Let me recognize you at that virginal point in the depth of my heart where you dwell and heal me.

*Nouwen,* A Cry for Mercy

The Presence then comes so close that you can sense it. On the wintry landscape, the searcher hears psalms sung, sees pilgrim bands, smells the incense of restored prayer, touches the company of the faithful, and even tastes.

*Marty,* A Cry of Absence

# New Horizons

There is no magic formula for attaining the emotional healing and spiritual peace so many people have found in the midst of adversity. For some it comes gradually, and for others it comes quite suddenly and unexpectedly. But no matter how it comes, those who have experienced it verify it is worth striving for and that it can happen regardless of outward circumstances.

*Hanner et al.,* When You're Sick and Don't Know Why

If we allow aching to teach us, and bear it in trust, then we can come through to its other side. There, even if the ache remains, it is more light, spacious, free, and wise. There the sun shines through it; the ache is shaken off center stage to the shadowy fringe.

*Tilden Edwards,* Living Simply through the Day

Difficulties are God's errands; and when we are sent upon them we would esteem it a proof of God's confidence—as a compliment from him.

*H. W. Beecher*

The great thing in this world is not so much where we are, but in what direction we are moving.

*Oliver Wendell Holmes*

We must always change, renew, rejuvenate ourselves; otherwise we harden.

*Goethe*

There is much to be said about the importance of attitude in dealing with one's cancer. It refers mostly to a state of mind. A life filled with love and laughter will get you through. That, and imagery. See your body killing off the cancer. It comes down to fighting the enemy with your mind and emotions.

*George Sheehan, M.D.,* Going the Distance

Help me to be thankful, God, for all the good things in my life and not take them for granted. And when things go wrong, help me not to be too sorry for myself but to remember so many other people whose lives are much harder: people who are always hungry, who are sick with no one to care for them, who have ability but no chance to learn. Help me to pray for them and forget myself.

*Avery Brooke,* Plain Prayers for a Complicated World

The longer we dwell on our misfortunes, the greater is their power to harm us.

*Voltaire*

I can't discount the power of love and prayers. I will always be grateful for what faith I had and for the love and prayers offered by many dear friends and family members. Several studies have shown that patients who pray or are prayed for heal faster and have fewer complications.

*Hanner et al.*, When You're Sick and Don't Know Why

Do not despise your situation; in it you must act, suffer and conquer. From every point on earth we are equally near to heaven and to the infinite.

*Henri F. Amiel*

If you're feeling particularly bitter, despairing, or angry, then the book of Job might be a good companion for your misery and help you get through it.

*Edwards,* Living Simply through the Day

Patience is a bitter plant, but it bears sweet fruit.

*German proverb*

We creatures are always being subjected to little nicks and bruises, pimples and bug bites, and besieged by hordes of alien bacteria and viruses. Some part of us is always in the process of healing. Consequently, the condition of health is not a static state of perfect wellness; it is, among other things, a condition of ongoing healing.

*M. Scott Peck, M.D.,* A World Waiting to Be Born

Fortify yourself with contentment, for this is an impregnable fortress.

*Epictetus*

A merry heart doeth good like a medicine: but a broken spirit drieth the bones.

*Proverbs 17:22, KJV*

When I am resting in green pastures, beside the still waters, I may not realize that I need God. But when life becomes turbulent . . . I need to know that "You are with me in the valley of the shadow."

*Kushner,* Who Needs God

[A] workable and effective way to meet and overcome difficulties is to take on someone else's problems. It is a strange fact, but you can often handle two difficulties—your own and somebody else's—better than you can handle your own alone. That truth is based on a subtle law of self-giving or outgoingness whereby you develop a self-strengthening in the process.

*Norman Vincent Peale*

One ought never to turn one's back on a threatened danger and try to run away from it. If you do that, you will double the danger. But if you meet it promptly and without flinching, you will reduce the danger by half. Never run away from anything. Never!

*Sir Winston Churchill*

Be of good courage, all is before you, and time passed in the difficult is never lost. . . . What is required of us is that we love the difficult and learn to deal with it. In the difficult are the friendly forces, the hands that work on us.

*Rainer Maria Rilke*

I will take away sickness from among you.

*Exodus 23:25*

# THE
# TROUBLES
# THAT
# AFFLICT US

# Coping with Illness

Sufferers of physical illness know that it has a way of working itself out with this rhythm of attack, relief, and new attack.

*Martin E. Marty,* A Cry of Absence

At about the same time as my cancer appeared, I heard a former United States senator tell of his reaction on learning he had a malignancy. He had resigned from the Senate, but not for medical reasons. He could have finished his term satisfactorily, but his reason for leaving was the heightened awareness his malignancy had given him. He had reexamined his life and then determined to live it in a different way. He discovered that the people in his life were more important than his cancer.

*George Sheehan, M.D.,* Going the Distance

When they saw Job's plight they were flabbergasted. They hardly knew what to think. The man whom they had known as the greatest man in their part of the world was ill and sitting on an ash heap. They were silent for seven days, having no comfort to give him. They said nothing and apparently Job said nothing in all that time . . . finally at the end of seven days Job opened his mouth and cursed his day.

*Theodore H. Epp,* Job, A Man Tried As Gold

When you hid your face, I was dismayed. To you, O LORD, I called; to the Lord I cried for mercy: . . . Hear, O LORD, and be merciful to me; O LORD, be my help.

*Psalm 30:7-8, 10*

Mark's spirits soared. Once again he felt God had answered his prayers by easing his discomfort and giving him something to anticipate. And he was further heartened in the days and weeks that followed with a steady stream of letters from people who . . . were writing to say they were praying for us.

*Shireen Perry with Gregg Lewis,* In Sickness and in Health

I only smile with my right side. My left side doesn't go up, but I can push it up with my hand. I wish I could smile right. I think that when I'm smiling, my left side is sleeping and dreaming of trying to smile.

*Katie Martin, in* I Will Sing Life

Grant to me O, Lord, the spirit of faith and courage, that I may have strength to meet the days to come with steadfastness and patience—not sorrowing as those without hope, but in thankful remembrance of your great goodness, and in joyful expectation of eternal life with those I love. This I ask in the Name of Jesus, who died and rose from the dead that those who believe in him might live forever. Amen.

The Book of Common Prayer, *paraphrased by Carl G. Carlozzi*

The return to health may involve a longer road for some persons than others, depending on how well balanced a person was to begin with. Any difficulties that existed before a stroke may be aggravated, at least during the early stages of readjustment. The physical history of the individual has to be taken into account. A person who has developed a variety of coping skills has an advantage over someone who is unprepared by experience to deal with crisis.

*Edgar N. Jackson,* Conquering Disability

Sometimes I suspect that great art—music, painting, poetry—is only born out of great pain, the sort of pain that shatters your old self, your old world-view, and compels you to give birth to a new one.

*Harold Kushner,* Who Needs God

God doesn't choose you to be sick. You just go outside and catch something or eat off the floor, or it's cold. But he helps when you do get sick.

*Sharon Valdez, in* I Will Sing Life

Propped up in bed, still far too weak to get up, but dressed for company in his gray Japanese happy coat with red Japanese lettering, Mark lifted his hands and sang song after song with his friends.

*Perry with Lewis,* In Sickness and in Health

I waited patiently for God to help me; then he listened and heard my cry. He lifted me out of the pit of despair, out from the bog and the mire, and set my feet on a hard, firm path and steadied me as I walked along. He has given me a new song to sing, of praises to our God. Now many will hear of the glorious things he did for me, and stand in awe before the Lord, and put their trust in him.

*Psalm 40:1-3, TLB*

Sometimes I suspect that the Psalms that move me most were not written by people of serene, untroubled faith but by people who had to struggle to find where God was hidden in their lives, not by people to whom God was obvious but by people for whom God was the reward at the end of a long and arduous search.

*Kushner,* Who Needs God

When I was able to stop focusing on my own feelings of rejection and fear and began to concentrate on coping with my illness, my sense of well-being improved. I searched my soul and learned just how much I wanted to be healthy. Yet I was powerless to change my circumstances or anyone else's opinion. I found a sense of inner peace and realized my ability to find joy in life in spite of them.

*Linda Hanner et al.,* When You're Sick and Don't Know Why

As a physician, I do not like unnecessary pain. I hate it. But we shall continue to suffer it egregiously until we learn to distinguish far more clearly between that pain which is indeed needless and that which is essential for our healing. This is because much disease is actually the result of the attempt to avoid the necessary pain of living and the frequent need for repair.

*M. Scott Peck, M.D.,* A World Waiting to Be Born

The great spiritual achievements may be wrought out in the quiet hours when you exercise the courage to be entirely honest with yourself, and when you develop the skills that come with practicing the courage to bring life to its spiritual optimum. You and you alone have the relationship with your own spiritual being to turn your rocky Patmoses into your personal Apocalypses. You can be thankful that your trials, with God's help, have given you mastery of life and have allowed you to grow spiritually.

*Jackson,* Conquering Disability

Now it matters not whether poverty or prosperity, sickness or health, peace or war, laughter or weeping, loneliness or popularity, failure or success, make up the warp and woof of life. Behind every thread in the tapestry of our days one senses the gentle hand of our heavenly Father fashioning a pattern of unique worth and beauty.

*W. Phillip Keller,* Taming Tension

# From Allergies to Ulcers

The heart attack occurred in my sixty-fifth year, and it taught me a great deal about the essential robustness of the human body and, in particular, how even a badly damaged heart can repair itself.

*Norman Cousins,* Head First, the Biology of Hope

If the day ever comes when I can't run, I shall walk. When I can't walk, I shall sit in a chair and smell the wind. And when I can't sit up any more, I shall lie on my back and watch the clouds once again.

*Robert Farrar Capon,* Health, Money, and Love . . . And Why We Don't Enjoy Them

It was then, in the quiet tent camps which I occupied alone in the African bush, that there began to dawn on me that it was tension, anxiety, worry, and stress which were in fact destroying me. It was there under the spreading acacia trees in the foothills of Mount Kilimanjaro, and later on the sands of a quiet Canadian beach that I began to believe my body could beat the damage done to it. And it did.

*Keller,* Taming Tension

In an hour it will still throb. In a day it will wane. In a month it will scar. In a year it will fade.

*Helen Elaine Lee, "Silences," in* Children of the Night, *edited by Gloria Naylor*

I am no longer the athlete I was. There is a tremendous difference between being sick and being well. In dramatic terms my play has to take this change into account. My life is not ready-made. I must make it myself.

This new life is strange to me. My old lifestyle was such that if I wasn't holier than thou, I was certainly healthier than thou.

*Sheehan,* Going the Distance

I never thought of being tied to bed all day long. I had expected to be strengthened to ignore or tread under foot bodily ills, and . . . to pass on straight from the midst of things without giving anyone any trouble.

*Carmichael,* Rose from Brier

Mark also shared . . . talking about his recent battle with depression, and letting people know he'd welcome phone calls during the day when he tended to be at his emotional low point.

*Perry with Lewis,* In Sickness and in Health

Guilt both real and imagined strikes at human beings in many disguises. It may be mental illness or physical illness. It may be a combination.

*Will Oursler,* The Healing Power of Faith

Think how aggressive we are in treating illnesses we consider physical, and yet we avoid treating those disorders that distort our emotions and mental capabilities. Fear and suspiciousness abound. This is a hurdle that must be gotten over. Millions are affected by this newly defined "spectrum" of illnesses. Most are living lives that are limited, if not filled with pain. But once properly diagnosed and treated, we can move on surprisingly quickly to fuller lives—lives that are energetic, creative, and enhanced by the wonder of existence.

*Colette Dowling,* You Mean I Don't Have to Feel This Way?

If the doctor ever did come, he would tell us that Mother was wrong when she said that we caught colds from running outdoors on nasty days. We probably caught them indoors, where the cold virus travels best, and we may even have caught them from Grandma, who liked to kiss us while reminding us to put on our earmuffs and galoshes.

*Bill Cosby,* Childhood

Most of us have been conditioned to expect dramatic results when it comes to health care. On TV, even obscure diseases are diagnosed and treated in 60 minutes—minus commercials! Wouldn't it be nice if that were true in real life.

*Hanner et al.*, When You're Sick and Don't Know Why

From the moment I discovered the lump, my life was never the same.

*Carolyn D. Runowicz, M.D., and Donna Haupt,* To Be Alive

I can remember, at the time, feeling very odd, as if it were only I who had such symptoms—as if everyone else in my family were solid as oaks and I was in some way flawed, a fragile shrub that might not survive the winter.

*Dowling,* You Mean I Don't Have to Feel This Way?

Pain was the ally it is designed to be, my body's way of insisting that something must change.

*Arthur Frank,* At the Will of the Body

The highest exercise of a physician's skills is to prescribe not just out of a little black bag but out of his or her knowledge of the human healing system.

*Cousins,* Head First, the Biology of Hope

During those first few months after treatment, you may find it hard to envision a time when cancer will not be your first thought when you awaken and your last thought before you fall asleep. But a time does come when cancer takes a backseat in your life, when the intense memories of therapy and the emotions surrounding it fade with time, and life can be enjoyed for its smaller pleasures.

*Runowicz and Haupt,* To Be Alive

Concentrate on what does help, whether it's counseling, taking care of yourself by resting and eating right, eliminating as much stress as possible, finding a doctor you trust and work with, or all of these.

*Hanner et al.,* When You're Sick and Don't Know Why

# Spiritual and Emotional First Aid

Survivors . . . can teach others an important lesson. . . . Life is a precious and magical gift to be lived in the fullest sense each and every day. Sure, there are darker moments when each woman loses self-confidence and begins to despair. But somehow these survivors have learned to take pleasure in the smaller, more common moments in life—not just the memorable occasions—and have found a sense of purpose and enjoyment to their lives no matter how long they last.

*Runowicz and Haupt,* To Be Alive

Why not learn to enjoy the little things— there are so many of them.

*Anonymous*

Until one has claimed a blessing from one's pain, one cannot be freed from it.

*Martin Israel,* The Pain That Heals

We are told that by faith all things are possible.

*Oursler,* The Healing Power of Faith

I needed the reassurance that there was a God out there someplace, who not only knew me by name, but who would also act in my behalf.

*William M. Kinnaird,* The Promise of Hope

I have learned through the faithfulness of Jesus Christ that there is a God who delights in restoring broken people to wholeness. That for me is the promise of hope.

*Kinnaird,* The Promise of Hope

When God allows a burden to be put upon you, he will put his arms underneath you to help you carry it.

*Anonymous*

The ability to rise above despair is one of the triumphs of the human spirit. After periods of disappointment and depression there comes the time of rebound and new hope. The momentum of life seems to carry us beyond times of low spirits.

*Jackson,* Conquering Disability

Don't let your sorrow come higher than your knees.

*Swedish proverb*

It is almost impossible to smile on the outside without feeling better on the inside.

*Anonymous*

It is paradoxical that sickness is the way to healing and suffering the path to wholeness.

*Israel,* The Pain That Heals

The ultimate value of illness is that it teaches us the value of being alive; that is why the ill are not just charity cases, but a presence to be valued.

*Frank,* At the Will of the Body

Dear Lord, by the power that went out from you a woman was healed of an illness no doctor had been able to cure and a young girl was called to life. You revealed that God is the God of life, in whom no death can be found.

*Henri Nouwen,* A Cry for Mercy

The art of living lies not in eliminating but in growing with troubles.

*Bernard M. Baruch*

Becoming the most that we can be is also the definition of salvation. The term literally means "healing." As we apply "salve" to our skin to heal it, so we can learn to apply the principles of mental health in our lives to heal, to make us whole . . . individually and collectively.

*Peck, M.D.,* A World Waiting to Be Born

You can't do anything about the length of your life, but you can do something about its width and depth.

*Evan Esar, quoted in* Good Advice

My religious perspective offers me the assurance that, though my body will one day give out, the essential Me will live on, and if I am concerned with immortality of that sort, I should pay at least as much attention to my soul, my nonphysical self, as I do to my weight and blood pressure.

*Kushner,* Who Needs God

# Practical Prescriptions

I am always content with what happens; for I know that what God chooses is better than what I choose.

*Epictetus*

He who suffers, remembers.

*Cicero*

Too often, patients who come to the end of an examination will feel they are missing something if the doctor fails to give them a prescription or place a bottle of pills in their hands. Pills have become what a patient expects in return for going to seek help.

*Benson with Proctor,* Beyond the Relaxation Response

Endure and persist; this pain will turn to your good.

*Ovid*

The best way to cheer yourself up is to try to cheer somebody else up.

*Mark Twain*

Make a list of the things for which you are grateful, and try to focus on them, especially when negative emotions begin crowding your mind.

*Memorial Hospital staff, Chattanooga, TN,* "Chicken Soup"

Do not anticipate trouble, or worry about what may never happen. Keep in the sunlight.

*Benjamin Franklin*

The longer I live, the more keenly I am aware that basically all that counts in life is what we can contribute of comfort, cheer, and inspiration to others. The success of our living is measured . . . by what we can bestow upon our fellow travelers on life's tough trail.

*Keller,* Taming Tension

When you encounter difficulties and contradictions, do not try to break them, but bend them with gentleness and time.

*Saint Francis de Sales*

Accustom yourself to that which you bear ill, and you will bear it well.

*Seneca*

God is never too late in coming to our aid but is always on time. In our impatience we may think there has been a delay, but in reality God always acts at the right moment.

*Epp,* Job, A Man Tried As Gold

You gain strength, courage and confidence by every experience in which you really stop to look fear in the face. You are able to say to yourself, "I have lived through this horror. I can take the next thing that comes along." You must do the thing you think you cannot do.

*Eleanor Roosevelt*

Friendship is good medicine.

*Memorial Hospital staff,* "Chicken Soup"

We should pray for a sane mind in a sound body.

*Juvenal*

We so seldom try to see what the other person sees. Perhaps we can look over the heads of the crowd, but our friend or neighbor is limited to a view of backs. We may have our life relatively put together and see bright skies. Our neighbor is suffering and sees only dark clouds.

All of us would be more humane and empathetic persons if we would at least try to see life from another person's viewpoint.

*Kinnaird,* The Promise of Hope

If thou would'st be borne with, then bear with others.

*Thomas Fuller*

Always laugh when you can. It is cheap medicine.

*Lord Byron*

Any battle with serious illness, I said, involved two elements. One was represented by the ability of the physicians to make available to patients the best that medical science has to offer. The other element was represented by the ability of patients to summon all their physical and spiritual resources in fighting illness.

*Cousins,* Head First, the Biology of Hope

With every haunting trouble then, great or small, the loss of thousands or the lack of a shilling, go to God. . . . If your trouble is such that you cannot appeal to him, the more need you should appeal to him!

*George MacDonald*

It is a mistake to try to look too far ahead. The chain of destiny can only be grasped one link at a time.

*Sir Winston Churchill*

Being ill is a perpetual balancing of faith and will.

*Frank,* At the Will of the Body

I have watched how many people turn cancer into a gift. It rallies some to a cause, and they become an invaluable support person or advocate. Others use cancer as a motivator to awaken them to enjoy life and the people around them, to value each day.

*Pam Collins, Memorial Hospital,* "Chicken Soup"

# SONGS AND SUNSHINE FOR THE SOUL

# The Promise of Healing

God desires to heal you! Mercy and healing are our heavenly Father's nature.

*Carl G. Carlozzi,* Promises and Prayers for Healing

Peace, peace to them, both near and far, for I will heal them all.

*Isaiah 57:19, TLB*

Who needs God?
I know I do.
I know we do.

*Harold Kushner,* Who Needs God

I wish to live because life has within it that which is good, that which is beautiful, and that which is love. Therefore, since I have known all of these things, I have found them to be reason enough and—I wish to live. Moreover, because this is so, I wish others to live for generations and generations and generations and generations.

*Lorraine Hansberry,* To Be Young, Gifted and Black

Living is a constant process of deciding what we are going to do.

*José Ortega y Gasset*


There is a time for everything,
and a season for every activity under heaven:
   a time to be born and a time to die,
   a time to plant and a time to uproot,
   a time to kill and a time to heal.

*Ecclesiastes 3:1-3*


While he was on earth, Jesus healed many who were ill and afflicted,
forgiving their sins and freeing them from their pain and distress.

*Carlozzi,* Promises and Prayers for Healing


One Sabbath as he was teaching in a synagogue, he saw a seriously
handicapped woman who had been bent double for eighteen years and
was unable to straighten herself.

   Calling her over to him Jesus said, "Woman, you are healed of your
sickness!" He touched her, and instantly she could stand straight. How
she praised and thanked God!

*Luke 13:10-13,* TLB

I'm so glad that Jesus lifted me,
I'm so glad that Jesus lifted me,
I'm so glad that Jesus lifted me,
Singing glory, hallelujah, Jesus lifted me.

*Traditional*

Be not afraid of life. Believe that life is worth living, and your belief
will help create the fact.

*William James*

I totalled my stress points one time and they were astronomical. By
all reason I should have been dead of a heart attack, or at least
should have had a bleeding ulcer or colitis. But I remained relatively
healthy. Why?

The only thing I can figure is that, because of Jesus Christ, I never
totally lost hope. My supply was dangerously low at times, but through it
all I believed Jesus Christ could rescue me. I'll have to be honest,
though, and say I wasn't always sure He would. The knowledge that He
could is what kept me going. That is what prevented total despair. I
always had hope. That was my built-in immunity.

*William M. Kinnaird,* The Promise of Hope

Do you really believe what He says is true?
Do you really believe it applies to you?
Does His Spirit testify
What your spirit cannot deny?
Faith is what you hope for, but you cannot see;
Faith is a conviction that what He says will be.

*James Ward, "Faith Is What You Hope For"*

O Lord who lends me life, lend me a heart replete with thankfulness.

*William Shakespeare*

Circumstances are the rulers of the weak;
they are but the instruments of the wise.

*Samuel Love*

It is when you are sick that you make the best plans to keep healthy.

*O. A. Battista,* Quotoons

Come, and let us return unto the Lord: for he hath torn, and he will heal
us; he hath smitten, and he will bind us up.

*Hosea 6:1, KJV*

With a cut . . . the doctor cleans the wound, puts the cut edges side by side in their natural place, and puts on a bandage to give it rest. That is what we can do for people: provide an environment that clarifies, cleanses, and lightens whatever messy situation is there, brings together what is torn asunder, and gives secure room for rest. This environment doesn't "make" healing happen. It allows it to happen.

*Tilden Edwards,* Living Simply through the Day

Necessity can set me helpless on my back, but she can't keep me there; nor can four walls limit my vision.

*Margaret Fairless Barbar*

The miracles of Jesus were the ordinary works of his Father, wrought small and swift that we might take them in.

*George MacDonald*

If you believe, you will receive whatever you ask for in prayer.

*Matthew 21:22*

# Heartfelt Courage and Endurance

Don't be impatient. Wait for the Lord, and he will come and save you! Be brave, stouthearted and courageous. Yes, wait and he will help you.

*Psalm 27:14, TLB*

God knows what we are and what we can endure; he will not allow us to be tested beyond our ability. He knows our temperaments and dispositions. He knows our various characteristics, our strong points and weak points; therefore he knows what to allow in our lives.

*Theodore H. Epp,* Job, A Man Tried As Gold

Praise can heighten your awareness that distressing circumstances are God's blessings in disguise. Your trials rip away the flimsy fabric of your self-sufficiency. This makes room for God's Spirit to weave into your life a true and solid confidence—the kind of confidence that Paul expressed in Philippians 4:13: "I can do all things through Christ who strengthens me."

*Ruth Myers,* 31 Days of Praise

Why are you so buckled over deep down?
And why are you groaning within me?
Can't you hope in God?
The One who keeps me safe—
I'll be praising him again sometime.

James Ward, "Buckled Over"

A bold and intrepid courage is at best but a holiday-kind of virtue to be seldom exercised, and never but in cases of necessity; mildness, patience, tenderness, good nature, are of daily use; they are the bread of mankind, the staff of life.

John Dryden

Patience is the best remedy for every trouble.

Plautus

The waves of adversity shatter on the rocks of courage.

Anonymous

Although I never discovered a formula for dealing with pain, I did manage to break through its incoherence one night before it abated. Making my way upstairs, I was stopped on the landing by the sight—the vision really—of a window. Outside the window I saw a tree, and the streetlight just beyond was casting the tree's reflection on the frosted glass. Here suddenly was beauty, found in the middle of a night that seemed to be only darkness and pain. Where we see the face of beauty, we are in our proper place, and all becomes coherent.

*Arthur Frank,* At the Will of the Body

Give us grace and strength to forbear and to persevere.

*Robert Louis Stevenson*

Lord, I've been down so long,
Down don't worry me.

*Spiritual*

We must always remember that God is in complete control in our suffering.

*Epp,* Job, A Man Tried As Gold

So let us praise Him now, though it may be from under the harrow, from the depths, from anywhere.

*Amy Carmichael,* Rose from Brier

When you get in a tight place and everything goes against you, till it seems as if you could not hold on a minute longer, never give up then, for that's just the place and time when the tide will turn.

*Harriet Beecher Stowe*

Prayers are no superstition; they are more real than the acts of eating, drinking, sitting, or walking.

*Mohandas K. Gandhi*

There was given me a thorn in my flesh, a messenger of Satan, to torment me. Three times I pleaded with the Lord to take it away from me. But he said to me, "My grace is sufficient for you, for my power is made perfect in weakness."

*2 Corinthians 12:7-9*

Give thanks for the grace there beyond our control or understanding. Grace isn't the same as healing. We want healing. We hope and pray for it. But grace is beyond healing. Grace is always there, simply present, through everything, whether or not it takes the form of that healing we want.

*Edwards,* Living Simply through the Day

I do believe . . . that God can bring good out of the worst of tragedies. While He may not have caused them (or "allowed" them, as some people put it), that still does not leave Him helpless. In fact, I think one of the greatest aspects of God's majesty is that He can bring good out of evil. His bodily Resurrection is evidence enough of that. There are "resurrections" going on all the time, resurrections of hopes and dreams—new life where hope was dead and buried.

I think if we look more to the possibilities that can come out of tragedy than to assigning the cause of it, we will all be more at peace.

*Kinnaird,* The Promise of Hope

Give us thankful hearts for all Your mercies. There is a wideness in Your mercy like the wideness of the sea!

*Jo Petty,* Golden Prayers

# Embracing the Dance of Life

Life, of course, is not without risk.

*Hugh Downs,* Perspectives

We must seek faith within ourselves. We must not be afraid to probe ourselves, our motives, our conscience, our understanding, our needs. For faith is not mere wish, it is not a dream, it is not running from reality. It comes by a probing of ourselves and our innermost meanings.

*Will Oursler,* The Healing Power of Faith

Celebration brings joy into life, and joy makes us strong.

*Richard J. Foster,* Celebration of Discipline

The joy of the Lord is your strength.

*Nehemiah 8:10*

Once you learn the true nature of health, you have room to expand your consciousness, to reach for personal greatness, or just to wave your arms in happy abandon if that suits your mood. You are finally free of the constricting idea that health is something you get in a drug packet, or as a reward for allowing a doctor to operate on you. The power to be healthy, you finally realize, is largely in your own hands.

*Robert Rodale,* The Best Health Ideas I Know

One of the precious realities of our Christian walk is that God cares for the simple, ordinary, day-to-day things of life.

*R. Kent Hughes,* Abba Father

Remember you are in the presence of the Most High God. He gives you breath. He holds your pulsing heart between his fingers. . . . He welcomes you with love. Let your rejoicing then be with reverence and with godly fear.

*John White,* Daring to Draw Near

Everything is an affair of the spirit.

*George MacDonald*

Thank God for inventing pain! I don't think he could have done a better job. It's beautiful.

*Philip Yancey,* Where Is God When It Hurts?

In my trials, Lord, walk with me;
In my trials, Lord, walk with me;
When my heart is almost breaking, Lord,
I want Jesus to walk with me.

*Traditional*

And since it is through much tribulation that we enter into the kingdom,
may we rejoice in all our sufferings which You allow.

*Petty,* Golden Prayers

To live is like to love—all reason is against it, and all healthy instinct
for it.

*Samuel Butler*

Would we really exchange anything for our health? Would we exchange
our sanity? Would you rather be healthy of body but paralyzed in mind,
or healthy in mind but paralyzed in body?

*Peter Kreeft,* Making Choices

The triumphal song of life would lose its melody without its minor keys.

*Anonymous*

Do not be anxious about anything, but in everything, by prayer and petition, with thanksgiving, present your requests to God. And the peace of God, which transcends all understanding, will guard your hearts and your minds in Christ Jesus.

*Philippians 4:6-7*

Celebration is a discipline. It is not something that falls on our head. It is the result of a consciously chosen way of thinking and living. As we choose that way, the healing and redemption of Christ will break into the inner recesses of our lives and relationships, and the inevitable result will be joy.

*Richard J. Foster,* Celebration of Discipline

There is always an indefinable something about people who have suffered. They have a fragrance which others lack.

*John R. W. Stott,* The Cross of Christ

## Bedside Blooms

It's your future. *Be There.*

*Advertisement in* Health, *May/June 1996*

Vaccinations are the safest, most effective little miracles in the already impressive bag of miracles possessed by modern science.

*Downs,* Perspectives

Many people are intimidated by doctors. They feel intimidated by them because they look busy and sound breathless all the time. People also feel stupid when they don't understand what a doctor's talking about the first time around, so they don't ask again. And let's be honest here, people. English is not a doctor's first language.

*Erma Bombeck,* I Want to Grow Hair, I Want to Grow Up, I Want to Go to Boise

Just because you have cancer, you are not different inside. You have to get out, find support, talk to other people with cancer, and reach inside for your own strength. Decide you are going to face cancer and not let it control your life. You can be in control of your own treatment, and most of all, fight, fight, fight!

*Pam Collins, Memorial Hospital,* "Chicken Soup"

My own grandmother, however, did know that nasty weather had not been the cause of a cold.

"Bill's got a cold," my mother would tell her.

"Is he regular?" she would reply.

Her entire view of life, in fact, was through the large intestine.

"Bill broke his arm," my mother would tell her.

"Is he regular?" she would reply.

To my grandmother, irregularity caused most of the problems in the world. She knew that the Japanese would never have attacked Pearl Harbor had they been mixing their rice with prunes.

*Bill Cosby,* Childhood

Without a doubt, becoming physically fit is one of the best—if not the best—of all health ideas. The results of a fitness program are quick and dramatic. If you use the right techniques, within a few days you will notice improvement in . . . your body, increase in your ability to work and enjoy life's pleasures, better resistance to stress and a more hopeful attitude toward life in general.

*Robert Rodale,* The Best Health Ideas I Know

So I pray: "Let me grow, in both health and illness, into the new me. Let me be worthy of the new me. Let me be thankful for the old me—for the old me was a gift, too—but keep me vulnerable. Let every part of me move toward the whole me."

*McFarland,* Now That I Have Cancer . . . I Am Whole

I never realized how resilient children are—how much physical pounding these small bodies can take and still come up smiling. Emotionally, they are like corks. Just when you think they are lost forever in the swirl of dark waters and rough seas, they surface to bob along innocently awaiting the next assault.

*Bombeck,* I Want to Grow Hair, I Want to Grow Up, I Want to Go to Boise

Working—or playing—through the flu is usually impossible, unless you're the type who can walk on hot coals and feel no pain.

*Jane E. Brody*

When you think about it, living is all about understanding and adjusting to things that occur, and arthritis is no exception.

*Dr. Doyt Conn,* Taking Care, *May 1996*

As I settled deeper into this new stage of my life, I became increasingly conscious of a certain thrill, an exhilaration even, about what I was doing. Yes, I felt pain, physical and psychological; but I also felt something like pleasure in responding purposefully, vigorously, to my illness.

*Arthur Ashe and Arnold Rampersad,* Days of Grace

People who feel healthy and who feel good about themselves tend to live more healthfully.

*Allen Luks with Peggy Payne,* The Healing Power of Doing Good

Keep your ideals high enough to inspire you, and low enough to encourage you.

*Anonymous*

Life without illness would not just be incomplete, it would be impossible.

*Frank,* At the Will of the Body

Even if you be healed by drugs (I grant you that point by courtesy), yet it behooves you to give testimony of the cure to God.

*Tatian*

I've always had the cool, silent determined courage of strength. Now I have the warm, bubbling, winging courage of weakness as well.

*McFarland,* Now That I Have Cancer . . . I Am Whole

Self-esteem can help you through a serious illness. . . . To build self-esteem . . . accept compliments, spend . . . time with people who appreciate your strengths, and recognize unfair criticism and do your best to disregard it.

*Dr. Elliot Frohman,* Taking Care, *May 1996*

Our happiness cannot be merely bodily health.

*Kreeft,* Making Choices

Aching certainly is not good in itself. But it is there. It can catch too neat, sleepy lives unawares, and, if we are attentive, shock us awake, becoming an unwanted but real means of grace.

*Edwards,* Living Simply through the Day

He won't fear no bad news,
Future will be bright.
'cause even in darkness light dawns
for the gracious and upright.

*James Ward, "No Bad News"*

# SOMETHING TO LIVE BY

# Help and Comfort

Teach us that we may serve You, Lord, even if with bent or broken tools.
*Jo Petty,* Golden Prayers

The LORD your God will . . . have compassion upon you.
*Deuteronomy 30:3*

True service . . . quietly and unpretentiously goes about caring for the needs of others. It puts no one under obligation to return the service. It draws, binds, heals, builds.
*Richard J. Foster,* Celebration of Discipline

As we give to others, we give also to ourselves—physically, emotionally, and spiritually.
*Allan Luks with Peggy Payne,* The Healing Power of Doing Good

When, after a painful illness, we have begun to recover, and have been able to stretch our limbs and open our eyes without pain, we have had comfort.
*Hannah Whitall Smith,* The God Who Is Enough

So now that I have cancer, it's okay just to be. Somehow I have permission from myself and the rest of the world to concentrate on this self, in order to get well. In the process, I have a chance not just to get cured, but to get whole, to be who I'm meant to be.

*John Robert McFarland,* Now That I Have Cancer . . . I Am Whole

"But how can God bring this about in me?"—Let Him do it and perhaps you will know.

*George MacDonald, "Righteousness," in* George Macdonald An Anthology, *by C. S. Lewis*

Jeanne and I kept my illness out of the news, where my name seemed to have been everywhere lately, at year's end. The honors and awards had come thick and fast. They pleased me, but they were not nearly as consoling as the visits of . . . friends, and the knowledge that people I have known for a lifetime were thinking about me and wishing me well.

*Arthur Ashe and Arnold Rampersad,* Days of Grace

When someone in a family is very sick, it is natural enough to hope that the illness will come to rest with that person. Rarely does this turn out to be the case. More likely the illness will ripple out, touching the lives of everyone.

*Colette Dowling,* You Mean I Don't Have to Feel This Way?

Sympathy is the result of thinking with your heart.

*Anonymous*

Come to me, all you who are weary and burdened, and I will give you rest.

*Matthew 11:28*

God wants us to bring our everyday needs to Him, even if they appear trivial. He doesn't demand that we approach Him only when we have raised ourselves to some kind of spiritual elevation above the everyday things of life. He comes to meet us where we are, and therein lies His greatness. When we come to Him with our "little things," we do Him great honor.

*R. Kent Hughes,* Abba Father

I must make it clear that you must never stop appealing to God about your sorrows and heartaches.

*John White,* Daring to Draw Near

I will not be afraid, for you are close beside me, guarding, guiding all the way.

*Psalm 23:4, TLB*

Caring has nothing to do with categories; it shows the person that her life is valued because it recognizes what makes her experience particular. One person has no right to categorize another, but we do have the privilege of coming to understand how each of us is unique. When the caregiver communicates to the ill person that she cares about that uniqueness, she makes the person's life meaningful.

*Arthur Frank,* At the Will of the Body

We cannot heal. We really cannot even help. All we can do is be patiently attentive: watching, being open, for the way grace might come through us in a situation.

*Tilden Edwards,* Living Simply through the Day

We are hard pressed on every side, but not crushed; perplexed, but not in despair.

*2 Corinthians 4:8*

There are huge wooden pieces of furniture, each with a brass plaque that expresses the thanks of the family who gave it as a gift. Many are dedicated to certain nurses. Others give thanks to everyone. One carries a poem:
　　When I needed help, you were there.

When I needed care, you cared.
I hope that when others are in despair,
They too find the love that was built into this chair.
God bless you.

*Belkin,* First, Do No Harm

Our Lord and the saints of the ages could pray during the storms because they had been praying in the sunshine. The could pray occasionally because they had also been praying continually. It is prayer's "whenever" nature that is the foundation for the special, emergency times—not the other way around.

*Steve Harper,* Praying through the Lord's Prayer

Jesus is the One who can walk on the water,
When things get dark and grim,
We can take His hand and stand in the storm,
With our eyes fixed on Him.

*James Ward, "Keep Looking Up"*

Hope is essential to keep the depths of despair from overcoming the courageous soul. . . . We would soon lose the incentive to try if always there was nothing but failure and defeat. The power of an undying hope shows through not because the sun is always shining, but rather because in times of darkness we have the faith to see the light shining in the future.

*Edgar N. Jackson,* Conquering Disability

May we trust in your power to heal.

*Petty,* Golden Prayers

# Patience and Peace of Mind

Patience, forbearance, and understanding are companions to contentment.

*Anonymous*

If each one of you will just enter into this relationship with Christ, and really be a helpless, docile, trusting sheep, and will believe Him to be your Shepherd, caring for you with all the love, and care, and tenderness that name involves, and will follow Him whithersoever He leads, you will soon lose all your old . . . discomfort, and will know the peace of God that passeth all understanding to keep your hearts and minds in Christ Jesus.

*Smith,* The God Who Is Enough

Somehow God gave me the grace to be patient. I was even able to write Mark to say: ". . . I won't abandon you. When you get well enough to come home, I'll be waiting."

*Shireen Perry with Gregg Lewis,* In Sickness and in Health

Through praise you focus your attention on God. You acknowledge Him as your source of overcoming power. You begin to look at your problems from a new perspective—you compare them with your mighty, unlimited God. You see them as molehills rather than mountains, as opportunities rather than hindrances, as stepping stones instead of stumbling blocks. You have a part in making them the prelude to new victories, the raw materials for God's miracles.

*Ruth Myers,* 31 Days of Praise

I am leaving you with a gift—peace of mind and heart! And the peace I give isn't fragile like the peace the world gives. So don't be troubled or afraid.

*John 14:27,* TLB

When the realization comes gently and assuringly to us that we are so designed as to cope with most diseases, a calmness and quietness settle over us. Gone is much of the tension and anxiety attached to our malady. For strange as it may seem, disease flourishes in the atmosphere of fear. Bodies break down more readily under tension. Anxiety actually augments and intensifies any attack made on the body.

*W. Phillip Keller,* Taming Tension

Cathie remains the caregiver whose affirmations mean the most to me. When it was becoming certain that I had cancer, she put her arms around me and told me she needed my survival, that her life required mine. I took the strength I needed from her and survived.

*Frank,* At the Will of the Body

Solitude may sometimes be integral to healing, a vessel in whose dark recesses new insights may germinate.

*Marc Ian Barasch,* The Healing Path

I feel better, so much better
Since I laid my burden down,
I feel better, so much better
Since I laid my burden down.

*Traditional*

There is only one place where we can receive, not an answer to our question, but peace—that place is Calvary. An hour at the foot of the Cross steadies the soul as nothing else can. "O Christ beloved, Thy Calvary stills all our questions."

*Amy Carmichael,* Rose from Brier

Faith is an attitude of will which says, "Whether I feel that God is there or not, whether I feel he will heed me or not, his Word tells me he hears and answers and I am going to count on that."

*White,* Daring to Draw Near

I quite humbly admit there are many blessings in life that can only be appreciated by those who have learned through their needs. I am glad I have learned these attitudes of life while there was yet time to practice them and enjoy the thankfulness that goes with them. I have learned much from my stroke and I have had many loving teachers.

*Jackson,* Conquering Disability

Let us run with patience the particular race that God has set before us.

*Hebrews 12:1,* TLB

Patience is so like fortitude that she seems either her sister or her daughter.

*Aristotle*

I have good days and bad days. The good days, thank goodness, greatly outnumber the bad. And the bad days are not unendurable.

*Ashe and Rampersad,* Days of Grace

Nothing happens to anybody which he is not fitted by nature to bear.

*Marcus Aurelius Antoninus,* Meditations

It has been a happy life. My limitations never make me sad. Perhaps there is just a touch of yearning at times. But it is vague, like a breeze among flowers. Then the wind passes, and the flowers are content.

*Helen Keller*

He who cares for the sparrows, and numbers the hairs of our head, cannot possibly fail us. He is an impregnable fortress into which no evil can enter and no enemy penetrate. I hold it, therefore, as a self-evident truth that the moment I have really committed anything into this divine dwelling place, that moment all fear and anxiety should cease.

*Smith,* The God Who Is Enough

There is no royal road to anything. One thing at a time, and all things in succession. That which grows slowly endures.

*Josiah Gilbert Holland*

Nothing great was ever done without much enduring.

*Catherine of Siena*

It is God's hand that propels us through life, even through storms, and accomplishes things for him.

*Hughes,* Abba Father

There is a balm in Gilead, to make the wounded whole,
There is a balm in Gilead, to heal the sin-sick soul.

*Traditional*

Patience is power; with time and patience the mulberry leaf becomes silk.

*Chinese proverb*

In God, whose word I praise,
In God I trust without a fear.

*Psalm 56:4,* RSV

# Timely Tips for Body and Soul

One has two duties—to be worried and not to be worried.

*E. M. Forster, The Observer, London, 20 Dec. 1959*

Life is an exciting business and most exciting when it is lived for others.

*Helen Keller*

Happiness is a result of the relative strengths of positive and negative feelings rather than an absolute amount of one or the other.

*Dr. Norman Bradburn, In Pursuit of Happiness*

Help one another, serve one another, for the times are urgent and the days are evil.

*Arthur Michael Ramsey, in The Hundredth Archbishop of Canterbury, by James B. Simpson*

When you think of a disease, you can think of the hospital. But when you think of an illness, you've got to think of home and family and community. Hospitals need to tie these together.

*Ron Anderson, M.D., in Healing and the Mind, by Bill Moyers*

Every new adjustment is a crisis in self-esteem.

*Eric Hoffer,* The Ordeal of Change

I think it's sometimes difficult for doctors, including myself, to understand why patients find it easier to accept a formidable diagnosis than no diagnosis at all.

*Linda Hanner et al.,* When You're Sick and Don't Know Why

I bandage, God heals.

*Ambroise Pare*

Surgery is always second best. If you can do something else, it's better. Surgery is limited. It is operating on someone who has no place else to go.

*Dr. John Kirklin*

One cannot be deeply responsive to the world without being saddened very often.

*Erich Fromm*

The greatest pain is that which you can't tell others.

*Yiddish proverb*

Doctors know that many of the patients who come to them complaining of headaches and stomachaches are actually suffering from depression. Their fleeting and sometimes not so fleeting disturbances have been described as "phantom" because in the past they were not thought to be grounded in anything organic.

Today researchers have a different idea about the bodily aches and pains that so often are a fact of depression.

*Dowling,* You Mean I Don't Have to Feel This Way?

Scripture commands us to live in a spirit of thanksgiving in the midst of all situations; it does not command us to celebrate the presence of evil.

*Richard J. Foster,* Celebration of Discipline

Good health does not take care of itself, and is most often lost by assuming that it will.

*O. A. Battista,* Quotoons

Maybe our ancestors were a little smarter than we are about some of these things. If you were the family doc, you lived down the street, and you knew what was going on. You knew the fact that the plant around the corner had laid off workers, and you knew whether certain problems in a patient were related to substance abuse. Even Native American medicine, which was a very effective form of health care, created a healing environment. And what we have to do now is reestablish a healing environment in our communities.

*David Smith, M.D., in* Healing and the Mind, *by Bill Moyers*

Miracles happen to those who believe in them.

*Bernard Berenson*

God raises the level of the impossible.

*Corrie ten Boom*

# The Wonder of Renewal

Fast from criticism, and feast on praise;
Fast from self-pity, and feast on joy;
Fast from ill-temper, and feast on peace;
Fast from resentment, and feast on contentment;
Fast from jealousy, and feast on love;
Fast from pride, and feast on humility;
Fast from selfishness, and feast on service;
Fast from fear, and feast on faith.

*Arthur Lichtenberger,* Anglican Digest, *Spring 1962*

Courage is a good word. It has a ring. It is a substance that other people, who have none, urge you to have when all is lost. To have courage, one must first be afraid. The deeper the fear, the more difficult the climb toward courage.

*Jim Bishop,* New York Journal-American, *March 14, 1959*

It is the body, not medicine, that is the hero.

*Glasser,* The Body Is the Hero

Life is something like this trumpet. If you don't put anything in it you don't get anything out. And that's the truth.

*W. C. Handy*

That is the God for me! He laid aside his immunity to pain. He entered our world of flesh and blood, tears and death. He suffered for us. Our sufferings become more manageable in the light of his.

*John R. W. Stott,* The Cross of Christ

How great is the love the Father has lavished on us, that we should be called children of God! And that is what we are!

*1 John 3:1*

God grant me
The serenity to accept the things I cannot change,
The courage to change the things I can,
And the wisdom to distinguish the one from the other.

*Reinhold Niebuhr*

I experienced that life was incredibly precious to me, and that the things that mattered most to me were my son and my wife. Driving down a highway at night, just looking at the fog—moment by moment, life was precious. I had that experience that so many people come here with, that the whole world has shifted and that they're seeing the world in a new way. It's an unfortunate fact that human beings learn through pain and suffering. If you ask yourself, have you learned most from the parts of your life that were easy, or the parts of your life that were painful, I imagine that like the rest of us, you've learned most from the parts of your life that were painful.

*Michael Lerner, quoted in* Healing and the Mind, *by Bill Moyers*

I would rather live in a world where my life is surrounded by mystery than live in a world so small that my mind could comprehend it.

*Harry Emerson Fosdick*

It gives me a deep comforting sense that "things seen are temporal and things unseen are eternal."

*Helen Keller*

Be of good courage, and he shall strengthen your heart, all ye that hope in the Lord.

*Psalm 31:24, KJV*

Day by day we should weigh what we have granted to the spirit of the world against what we have denied to the spirit of Jesus, in thought and especially in deed.

*Albert Schweitzer*

Taste and see that the LORD is good.

*Psalm 34:8*

To know that we are small yet accepted and loved, and that we fit into the exact niche in life a loving God has carved out for us is the most profoundly healthy thing I know.

*White,* Daring to Draw Near

May the Lord bless you real good!

*Billy Graham*

Oh, my Good Lord's done been here!
Blessed my soul and gone away,
My Good Lord's done been here,
Blessed my soul and gone.

*Traditional*

I know that I turn my back on God only at my peril. This I shall never do.

*Ashe and Rampersad,* Days of Grace

Everybody has pain, everybody is wounded. And because the participants can't cover up their woundedness, now that they have cancer, they can trust each other. You see, it's our woundedness that allows us to trust each other. I can trust another person only if I can sense that they, too, have woundedness, have pain, have fear. Out of that trust we can begin to pay attention to our own wounds and to each other's wounds—and to heal and be healed.

*Rachel Naomi Remen, M.D., in* Healing and the Mind *by Bill Moyers*

The shout of a steadfast faith is an experience that is in direct contrast to the moans of a wavering faith, and to the wails of discouraged hearts.

*Smith,* The God Who Is Enough

Dwell in the life and love and power and wisdom of God, in unity one with another and with God; and the peace and wisdom of God fill your hearts.

*George Fox*

Be, Lord,
within me to strengthen me,
without me to preserve me,
over me to shelter me,
beneath me to support me,
before me to divert me,
behind me to bring me back,
and round about me to fortify me.

*Lancelot Andrewes*

May the God of hope fill you with all joy and peace as you trust in him,
so that you may overflow with hope by the power of the Holy Spirit.

*Romans 15:13*